SUCCEED!

BECAUSE I FAILED

LEARN THE LESSONS OF FAILURE FROM SOMEONE WHO FAILED

Volume 1: Business Ownership

Copyright © 2023 by Josh Davis

Table of Contents:

Disclaimer:

The book you are about to read is my opinion about what NOT to do when you start a business or any significant project. These opinions are based on actual experiences that I went through.   It will become apparent when you read about my failures that I am NOT a business expert. None of my opinions should be believed as facts for every situation. Some things that didn't work for me may work for you. Some things that may have worked for me won't work for you. You know your business. Use this book as one of many informative research items you absorb and make the best decision possible for you and your family.

Introduction:

Hello, my name is J.D., and I am a failure.

In his book, Failing Forward, John Maxwell said best: "The difference between ordinary people and achieving people is their perception of and response to failure." Well...I took that to heart and lived my life by it. I have never been afraid to fail. Because of this mindset, I have accomplished as much as I have. I am a man of average-at-best intelligence and below-average-at-best looks. I was more of a B/C student in school. I was athletic but not the best athlete. I was just your typical average kid. One that would be easily forgettable if I just accepted life as it came to me.

I didn't just accept my limitations. I didn't just assume that this was the best I could do. In school, I would take challenging courses. These courses were way above my skill set and showed the high risk of failure, but they allowed me to stand out from my classmates. It got them to think of me like I was smart. I always asked out girls who were WAY out of my league. I took the chance of being turned down, and yes, that did happen...A LOT. But I always had the most beautiful dates to the prom and had two marriages to women who were so much better than me (Yes, I said two marriages, but that failure story will be in another book).

By the time I was 25, I had a couple of degrees from prestigious colleges; I had a great job making more than I ever thought I would be making, owned my own home, and had a beautiful family. Most people would have considered that I was doing well. Life was by no means perfect over the next ten years, but I always found ways to weather whatever storm that was ahead of me.

By the time I was 35, I had been through a divorce and remarried (again, this will be for another book), my career path was continuing to show a high trajectory towards the executive levels, I owned an even bigger house and fancy toys. At this point, people would have considered me as "Rich." I should have been content with my life. After all, I took many risks to get where I was, and I should be happy that I came out on top of most of those risks. I should have left well enough alone. I didn't.

I invite you to come with me as we go through one of my epic journeys to failure. One where all of the risks taken turned out differently than planned. One where the consequences of failure meant disaster for myself and my family.

One last thing of note. I want to make it very clear. I am not a writer. My grammar sucks. I'm sure I would receive a failing grade if I turned this in to any middle school English teacher. If you are looking for proper punctuation or a crisp, clean storyline, please do not

continue. This story is raw. This story is me.
However, if you are a business owner or an inspiring
business owner working hard to make it successful,
read on. Understand my failures and make the
necessary corrections that I failed to do. I want you to
be successful!

A Walk Through My Epic Failure:

My journey toward the biggest failure in business started with my near-death experience in 2018: February 5th, the Monday after my Philadelphia Eagles won their first Super Bowl. I had the day off work to continue celebrating, and by sheer coincidence, a big snowstorm came through, so the kids had off school. Not wanting to waste this opportunity to have fun with the kids and continue celebrating the bird's victory, we grabbed our snow tubes and hit our hill to have fun. Now, the hill at our house was not any normal hill. It was over 300ft long and steep. At the bottom of the hill was a snow fence that I put up just that year. On the other side of that snow fence was an 8ft cliff that led to the main road that goes by our house. I wanted to be the first to ride down to catch the other kids before they got too close to that fence. So on to the snow tube and down the hill I went. I didn't realize that below the 6 inches of fresh snow was a sheet of ice. I started picking up speed and tried to use my hands to stop, but it didn't work. As I hit the snow fence, the fence leaned toward the road. So, instead of the fence stopping me, it turned into a ramp that sent me flying over that 8ft cliff and landing me right onto the middle of that main road. Unfortunately, my tube decided not to make the journey onto the road, so the left side of my body smacked directly onto that hard, frozen road. God was looking out for me that day because there was no traffic on the road then. If there was, I could quickly have been struck by a car and killed. Instead, I did a barrel roll to the ditch until my wife could come down and get me to the emergency room. At the end of that day, I had a cracked skull, two cracked ribs, and a broken collar bone. I know I was lucky because it could have been much worse, but this did get me thinking about my future.

I knew that if I died, my family would get a good chunk of life insurance, but eventually, that money would be gone, and they would have to fend for themselves. I knew that I needed to create an income stream that would be able to produce if I was no longer around. I knew I needed to start my own company.

Starting my own company was not a spur-of-the-moment epiphany. It had been something that my wife and I discussed for a while. We had tossed around several ideas in the past, but the one that filled a need was a family entertainment center that provided activities for children all year round. The area we previously lived in had one of these entertainment centers, but the area we moved to didn't have anything for young children to do in the winter. We both knew it would be a hit if we opened a business like that, but my wife was busy with our young children, and I was already working 50 to 60 hours per week at my job. We didn't have the time to do it. I continued researching this business model, but that idea was always on the back burner until February 5th, 2018.

For the next three weeks, and with my arm in a sling, I put together a business plan for our company. I provided a detailed breakdown of all the services that our company would provide to the community. I did demographic research to see how many households had children within a 30-mile radius. I searched for a building that accommodated what we needed. I even provided forecasted financials that were calculated using industry standards. By the last week of February, I had a 78-page business plan that covered the company's details and provided a financial needs forecast to secure a business loan from the bank. In the first week of March 2018, I officially registered my LLC.

Things started moving quickly in March. I was able to come to a verbal agreement for a building to operate in. Knowing we had about three months' worth of construction to prepare the building, we decided on a lease start date of June 1st. I also got a business start-up loan approval from a local bank. Things were cooking, but there was one thing that was still bothering me. The fact is that I have never run a family entertainment business before.

So, I emailed the owner of the family entertainment center by our previous home to see if I could pay her for her time and pick her brain on how to run this type of business. We sat down to discuss and immediately hit it off. My ideas were very similar to how she was running her operation. By the end of the conversation, she asked me if I was interested in purchasing her company. This had never occurred to me before, but I thought there was no better way to learn to run this operation than to jump in with both feet. So, over the next month, we negotiated terms for the sale, and on June 1st, 2018, the same day we signed the lease for our original location, I purchased this business. This purchase was not part of the original business plan, and I did not have enough money to cover it in the start-up budget, but we worked out an owner-financing agreement, so I didn't need to use any of that money. Plus, based on the financials of that company, the revenue generated at that location should be enough to pay for itself.

As I mentioned, the lease to the future center and the purchase of the existing company were made official on June 1, 2018. In just 117 days, I went from sitting in front of my TV with my wife and kids, cheering the Eagles to a Superbowl Championship. To have a full-time career, owning an LLC company, operating an existing family entertainment center, and preparing the new family entertainment center for a September grand opening. To say that my plate was packed would be an understatement.

Except for a few hiccups on the construction side, summer 2018 went reasonably smoothly (Don't worry, I will discuss the hiccups further in this book). Our new location, which was set to be our flagship center, opened for business on September 8th, 2018. My wife and I had conversations about this area needing something like this, which proved spot on because people came from all around to enjoy our new space. The September launch time was perfect because it led right into the busy season (the Winter Months) for indoor family entertainment centers. From September until April 2019, I saw monthly revenue numbers higher than I predicted. There was little doubt we were the talk of the town.

With revenue numbers going up, so did our expenses. The problem was that the costs were outpacing even our highest revenues. Even when income was left over, I was quick to either purchase something new for the facility or keep the money and spend it on something personal for the family. So, by the time the busy season had ended in April, we had been unable to put away any money. We continued this trend of uncontrolled expenses and underperforming months through 2019. I lost a lot of money this year. I had to supplement the business revenues with my money to meet ends. Things will get better, though. I mean, 2020 has to be better than 2019. Right?

Oh COVID... The killer of dreams. This Pandemic impacted many businesses, and my company was no exception. Our state Governor forced us to close all operations in March 2020. The location I bought had to stay shut down through October 2020 and never recovered after re-opening. We remained at that location until March of 2022. We had to shut down because the mall we were located in was closing its doors. So, there is no more revenue from that location. The problem was that I still owed money to the previous owner as part of the sales agreement.

My primary location opened back up in June of 2020, but didn't see many participants that summer due to COVID still being an Impact. So I had little revenue owed money for a business that is not open anymore. I still had three years left on the lease for my primary location, no money in my business checking account, and very little in my checking accounts. The risks I had taken were starting to pile up on the failure side, but I was not about to say I quit. I sold all my stocks and invested money into the business to cover operating expenses. I also knew we needed to find a way to get additional revenue that didn't involve people leaving their homes because they were afraid to get sick. Understanding the current climate, I pivoted my strategy. While we remained open for any indoor customers we had, In July 2020, I started to bring the parties to the customer. I purchased four inflatable bounce houses from a company that closed permanently due to COVID and started an at-home rental service. That was me. Instead of taking that money and paying down debt, I took that money and bought inventory that may generate additional income but would create more work for me.

My company began to recover in 2021 and saw record revenue in 2022. Things started to look like 2023 may be the year I can get it all figured out and turn a profit. Not so fast! My 5-year lease was ending on May 31st, 2023. I met with the building owner, and my monthly rent expenses would increase by 50% for me to have a new lease. This increase was too much of a jump. I would have needed to raise high admission prices so parents would eventually be unable to afford it and stop coming. So, I, again, took a risk and decided not to renew my lease and look for a new location to operate. We shut down indoor operations on May 28th, 2023. The summer was the slow months anyway, so I decided to focus on renting the inflatables out while moving into a new location and relaunching the indoor side in September 2023. While the inflatable bounce house rental part was very strong, finding a suitable location for a new building proved harder than expected. I had verbal agreements with four different building owners to move my operations there. Only to have all four agreements fall through because the owners had a change of plans.

It's now September 2023. This was the month that I thought I would be reopening my indoor operations and using what I learned from my failures to get my business set up the right way to make a profit. Instead, I have no building, no indoor operations, my inventory in storage units, and soon-to-be no revenue since the rental season is ending. I still owe debts to 4 different entities for start-up loans and the purchase of the original business. These four debts are tied to my house and other personal guarantees. I assumed a lot of risk trying to be a business owner. These risks had the potential to lead to massive profits and financial security for my children's children. They also carried the potential of failure and the loss of everything.

Unfortunately, it was the latter that came true. I stand before you right now, a broken man. Someone who not only stands a high chance of losing all the physical stuff that I have worked for but also stands a chance of losing the wife and family that I let down.

I have learned from my failures with this experience. Right now, the issue is that I have no opportunity to use what I have learned from this epic failure to be able to make my company operate correctly. I kept asking myself what I would have done differently if I could start over again. Aside from not even opening a business, there would be a lot I would do differently. Even though I may not be able to benefit from everything my failures have taught me, who is to say someone else is sitting in the same position I was in 2018 and wondering what type of business they want to open? Could they skip making their own mistakes and learn from mine?

That is what this book is about. I will take you through the same story I just went through but through the eyes of failure. I will list each failure chronologically and provide additional details to explain what happened, why, and what I would have done differently. All I ask is that you take from my failures what you want. Some things that didn't work for me may work for you. You may be more intelligent or way more business savvy than me. This is not a book where I am boasting about my accomplishments. It's the exact opposite. I am embarrassing myself, laying all my failures on the table for you to see. I am doing this, hoping you do not repeat my mistakes. Instead, you leap over those pitfalls and deliver to your family what I could not deliver to mine.

Failure #1: Letting My Ego Dictate My Decisions:

I used to get annoyed when I heard people call me lucky for attaining the level of success I had. I thought I got to where I was through hard work, grit, and not fearing failure. I moved up quickly in my career because I didn't stay in the same company for long. Instead of waiting 4 or 5 years for an internal promotion, I would just get hired into that promotion role by another company after two years. I left companies I enjoyed for the chance at faster advancement and more money in positions I didn't know I would enjoy at companies I didn't know I would like. I took risks with these career moves. And these risks worked out in my favor. Most of the time, I could settle into my new role and do what needed to be done to impress my new bosses. That is, until it was time to move on to the next career move. While I was proud of my hard work ethic and not being afraid to take chances, I was also lucky enough to fall on the winning side of those chances. It turns out that the people who always called me lucky were right. During this time, I did not see it that way. I only saw how successful I had become through my own doing. I had created an over-inflated ego that honestly didn't think I could fail.

I wanted this to be the first failure I discussed because you will see it percolate in every chapter below. I was so conceited and sure of my abilities that I did not doubt that I would be able to make this company a huge success. Even though I had zero experience in business ownership and all the details that needed to be covered to start a business, I knew I could do it all myself. I told my family. I told my friends. All knew I was launching a new company. Even when my original revenue forecasts didn't look promising, and most people would have decided against launching the business, I pushed on. I wouldn't let my friends and family think I was a loser who couldn't start a company. No way! Come hell or high water, this company was going to launch.

My ego started writing checks that I was unable to cash. At this point, it didn't matter how much money I had to put into getting this company running; I was going to do it. I spent all my start-up loan funds and over $80,000 of my savings to be able to open the doors that September. When the business initially made massive revenue, we spent more than we were making due to mismanaging our controllable costs. I could have worked on a plan to pivot to a more conservative approach. Nope, not me. That would mean that I didn't know what I was doing. I just dumped more of my savings into the business. I was trying to spend my way to success.

This destructive circle continued into 2019. This year, I started running low on my savings and could not put much additional money into our business. Did I change course, then? Nope! I found two companies that would give me lumps of cash within 24 hours. To keep people from knowing how poor of a business owner I was, I chose to take $20,000 from these companies. All I had to do was pay them back $30,000 over four months. That's a 240% APR Interest Rate! I kept thinking that I was using these funds as a temporary solution. I was so sure I would figure it out. I was so sure I was going to find the secret sauce and be a success. I just needed a little more time to figure it out. There was no way I would let anyone see me start a business and have it fail in just two years. My ego would not let me make that decision.

When COVID hit in 2020, I was devastated. How will I dig out of this hole I put myself in and generate profit when the world is afraid to leave their homes? While COVID did put me through one of the worst years of my life, the ego in me did show some signs of relief. I remember thinking that I could now push the blame for our failing business on COVID. It wasn't years' worth of poor decisions and ego-driven choices that I made that got me here. It was COVID!

I had my out! No one would ever blame me for a business that failed during COVID. During the Summer of 2020, the owner of the building I was operating in sold his building to another investor. I was told that even though my lease was not up until 2023, I would be able to break my lease with no penalties or repercussions because of the change in ownership. I could have taken that option, applied for an SBA economic injury disaster loan, and used those funds to pay off most of my debt. I would still have my company but could focus on the more profitable rental side during the summer. A more stable person would have jumped all over this option. For me, this would have still meant defeat. Instead, I stayed in a building that was too costly for me to make any real profits and kept my legally binding lease intact for the entire five years.

You will see my ego play a massive part in all the chapters in this book. Confidence is essential in the business world, but you can't let your confidence rise so high that you think you can't fail. When faced with decisions, try to pull your desires and dreams of the outcome away. Look at problems objectively. Please seek advice from people who have done it before. If you don't, you will be like me. Sitting back, wondering what life would have been like if you decided the numbers weren't promising enough and chose not to launch a business that would ultimately leave you and your family embarrassed and broke.

DO NOT LET YOUR EGO DICTATE YOUR DECISIONS!

Failure #2: Planning for the Best Possible Outcome:

Mark Twain is credited with saying, "Figures don't lie, but liars figure." I have translated that to mean, "Numbers don't lie, but liars use numbers." I spent much time "crunching" numbers when writing my business plan to show a high-profit margin and a strong chance of success. Since I thought I was such a numbers master, I created a detailed spreadsheet that could pull all the data I collected and produce a financial forecast for the business. This was nothing more than guesswork. It sure looked pretty, however.

Using a mixture of industry standards from my research (also known as Google) and the information on what I would charge for things like admission, parties, food, etc. I created the financial projections below:

Industry Standard Revenue % to Total Revenue

Industry Standard % Admission Revenue	53%
Industry Standard % Party Revenue	15.50%
Industry Standard % Concession Revenue	0
Industry Standard % Merchandise Revenue	55%

Company Revenue Projections

Item	Custom Cost
Area Population	139,068
% of Population 2-12 Years Old	15.50%
Calculation of Population 2-12 Years Old	21,556
% of Children That Will Visit	55%
# of Unique Admissions	11,856
Projected # of Repeat Visits (Annually)	3.2
Total # of Children Admissions (Annually)	37,938
Average Price for Admission	$ 8.50
Annual Admission Revenue	$ 322,470.88
Annual Party Revenue	$ 235,361.28
Annual Concession Revenue	$ 37,848.04
Annual Merchandise Revenue	$ 9,431.77
Total Annual Revenue	$ 605,111.97

When I plugged in population numbers that I pulled from census reports and combined them with "Industry Standard" data around the percentage of children that would visit, my eyes got as big as saucers. I couldn't believe that almost 12,000 unique children would pay to come to my business and average over three return trips yearly. That's over 37,000 paid admissions every year! Then, seeing that admissions usually account for only 53% of the total revenue, I would get another $282,000 in revenue from parties, concessions, and merchandise. This calculator that I built (Since I was so clever) showed an annual income of over $600,000!

The revenue side of this plan was looking perfect! It's time to move on to my projected expenses:

Company Expenses

Item	Custom Cost
Marketing & Promotions	$ 5,000.00
Repairs & Maintenance	$ 6,000.00
Operating Supplies	$ 12,000.00
Utilities	$ 24,000.00
Insurance	$ 12,000.00
General Office & Admin	$ 10,000.00
Other	$ 5,000.00
Rent	$ 90,000.00
Employee Costs	$ 141,000.00
Total Annual Expenses	$ 305,000.00

With my extensive business knowledge (I hope you noticed the sarcasm), I figured we would be spending around $300,000 yearly in expenses. That seemed like a lot, but that would still leave me around $300,000 in profit annually. I also projected a need for about $200,000 in start-up funds, but with this profit margin, I would see a return on my investment in the first year. I mean, this is a no-brainer! At this point, I was thinking about quitting my full-time job and doing this. Yes, that's right, before we even opened the door and after looking at a spreadsheet I created, I already thought this could produce enough revenue to replace my full-time job.

You know the saying about if something sounds too good to be true, it usually is? Well, that is what I discovered about Industry Averages and Statistics. Our total number of Admissions in year one was around 15,000. We didn't hit the 38,000 mark that my numbers said we would until around 2020. If I had stopped drooling over the $235,000 in project party revenue, I might have realized that I needed to run almost 1,200 parties yearly to hit that revenue target. We would do around 350 parties in that first year for $70,000. My year one revenue came in around $275,000. A bit off from the $605,000 that my big brain and I had projected.

To compound my struggles, it turned out that I under-forecasted some of my expenses. I projected $24,000 for utilities. It turns out that 20,000 sqft buildings are quite expensive to heat and cool. I saw monthly electric bills ranging between $2,500 to $5,000. Monthly expenses like water, phones, and internet are added to my utility payments. By the end of year 1, my utilities expenses were over $40,000.

To sum that up, my revenue went down, and my expenses went up. That type of equation does not bode well for a business owner. I spent all my planning, dreaming about the best possible outcome that our business could have instead of creating a realistic plan for what our business would look like under normal circumstances. If I were doing this all over again, I would have taken my expectations and cut them by 75%. What would the business look like if I only made $151,000 in revenue yearly? Would I have picked the building we were in? Definitely no. Would I have decided there wasn't enough money to be made in this business and scrap the whole thing? Maybe so. Keeping my head out of the clouds and leaning more towards a pessimistic market would have made me more cautious and let me be pleasantly surprised by the higher-than-expected revenue instead of scratching my head about how it all went so wrong.

DO NOT PLAN FOR EVERYTHING TO WORK OUT! BE A LITTLE PESSIMISTIC

Failure #3: Bypassing LLCs by Using Personal Guarantees:

Disclaimer: This chapter briefly touches on some details around legal business formations. I discuss the type of legal formation I chose and why I chose that entity. This is not an endorsement or non-endorsement of any specific business formation. These are my opinions and my experiences. Please do your research to decide what's best for you.

In March 2018, when researching what type of company I wanted to start, I had several choices. I narrowed my decision to two possible formations: LLC or S Corp. I ultimately ended up choosing to be an LLC. The LLC or Limited Liability Company had two key factors that drove my decision. One was that an LLC for a single person (Sole Proprietorship) tends to be more flexible than a corporation around profit distribution. This flexibility was great for a guy with very little business sense, but the second point addressed the most significant issue I was nervous about. The Limited Liability Company could protect me from personal liability in business obligations.

Even though I never told anyone about this, I was so scared to open a family entertainment center because of the chance of being sued if a child would hurt themself at my facility. I envisioned a child twisting an ankle and his family suing me for millions of dollars. This lawsuit would be so high that I would lose my entire business, home, and possessions. This type of risk kept me up at night. So, when I understood how limited liability companies protected me from these types of lawsuits, I knew this was the kind of business I needed. Did I need to consult a tax professional to get their recommendation? No. Why would someone of my intelligence need to pay a CPA to give me the information I already knew? Remember, I can do this all by myself.

When my LLC was legally formed in March 2018, I was excited to move forward with my business plan without any legal recourse that could impact me or my family personally. I can now purchase that existing company that I wanted, get my start-up loan from the bank, and sign my lease for my future flagship location. Now it's time to start spending some money!

The next logical step that needed to be made was to secure my start-up loan. I drafted an extensive and detailed business plan, professionally printed and bound it, put on a fancy suit, and headed to the local community bank. This plan showed that I would need a start-up budget of $225,000. $50,000 of this budget would be provided from my savings. I asked that the remaining $175,000 be funded through a business loan to my LLC. The numbers in the business plan made sense, and the bank meeting went very well. They understood my vision and wanted to work with me on this project. Towards the end of this meeting, they asked me if I owned my own home. I said yes but thought this was weird because I had an LLC. Why would they need to know if I owned my home?

A couple of days after my meeting, I got a call from the bank and was informed that they would be willing to fund the $175,000 start-up need, but they would need to attach my home to the loan as a personal guarantee. I explained that I had an LLC and wanted the loan attached to my company. They told me that since my company has no proven financial history, they could only secure my funds with collateral to protect the bank. I didn't want to feel like I didn't know what I was talking about, so I just said, "OK." I gave the bank the financial information about my income and my home. The bank let me know that I did not have enough equity in my home to cover the entire amount that needed to be protected, so they could still not give me my loan.

At this point, I should have realized it might not be the best time to start a business financially. I should have looked at myself in the mirror, cut my minimal losses, and walked away. To me, walking away would have admitted defeat, and I DON'T LOSE! Instead of walking away, I asked my family for help. Not to ask for money. I knew that they didn't have a lot of money. Even though they didn't have much cash to be able to loan me, they both owned homes, and these homes had equity. On May 1st, 2018, I got my $175,000 loan deposited into my business account. All it took for my LLC, which is supposed to protect my assets, was a personal guarantee secured with my home and the homes of my mother and mother-in-law. That's right; my ego presented the business plan to two family members who would love and support me the most. When I signed my name to this loan, I might as well have bet my loved ones' financial security on a roulette wheel.

I received a sales contract for that existing company I planned to purchase. This purchase was seller-financed entirely. On this sales contract, everything the LLC owned secured the seller's finances, including my home address. My home address was included because the seller wanted a personal guarantee that this debt would be paid. Again, I thought that everything would go through my LLC. Since my LLC was only on paper and had no financial history, this seller needed security for the debt. While I was not happy with seeing my house on the line again for this business, my projections showed that the revenue it would generate would be able to cover the monthly price for this business. It's not like I will turn back now and give back that loan to the bank. That would mean I failed as a business owner. Everything was signed, and the sale was completed on June 1, 2018. So now I have a home mortgage with a 2nd mortgage from my business loan and a 3rd mortgage for purchasing this business.

June 1st was a busy day for me. On top of purchasing the existing business, I also signed my lease for my flagship business. This location was perfect! It was 20,000 square feet and in a great location. It needed a lot of work, but all I saw when I looked at this place was "Potential." I was given the lease document two weeks before signing so my lawyer could review it with me and we could come back with changes. Did I do this? Come on, I would think by now that you know this answer is "NO." I just read this lease myself. They used words like "Triple Net" and "Leasee Responsibility." I had to google much of this to find out what it all meant, but I felt I got the gist of the lease. One thing included in this lease was something that was beginning to be a repetitive requirement. The lease was issued to my LLC but also required a personal home guarantee. By this time, I assumed this was a standard inclusion to all loans and leases. I also thought I promised my home to three other entities; why not add a fourth? By the end of June 1st, I had over $12,000 in monthly debt or lease obligations tied directly to my positions via guarantees. I wish you could see how sick writing this stuff makes me.

With these actions, I bypassed all the protections I wanted the LLC to shield me from. I am not personally responsible for the business debt. What makes it even worse is that I took advantage of my mother's generosity and love and made them personally liable for a business they don't own. It's September 2023, and I no longer have a flagship building. I do not have the original business that I bought anymore. I still have my debt to the bank, to the original seller of that existing business, and to the building owner where my lease was signed. I have no revenue generation and over $6,000 in monthly payments for the debt. I am down to my last few options to pay off my debt. Either I find a buyer for my company that would have a setup to make it profitable, or I will need to sell my home and force my wife and kids through the humiliation of bankruptcy.

Looking back with clearer eyes, I see the requirements of personal guarantees as warning signs. Signs that should have steered me away from moving forward. I would not have moved forward with those deals without personal guarantees. I know that most agreements include this for new companies, but it is not worth putting my family through this fear and uncertainty.

I would not have purchased that existing business. I would have thanked that owner for the information they volunteered to give me but would have focused on launching my business correctly. I would have pulled back the need for a start-up loan and scaled down my business start-up so I could use my finances to launch. If I still needed funds that exceeded what I could personally put in, I would reach out and look for short-term investors. The reduction of the financial need would have resulted in over $7,000 in monthly expenses. Having that additional $84,000 each year, $426,000 in total, would have changed the fate of my company. Even if the results remained the same, even if my business is closed by September 2023, I would have no financial obligation to this company. I could suck up my losses and move on with my career, and my family would still have their house.

DO NOT GIVE PERSONAL GUARANTEES ON BUSINESS DEALS

Failure #4: Biting off More Than I Could Chew:

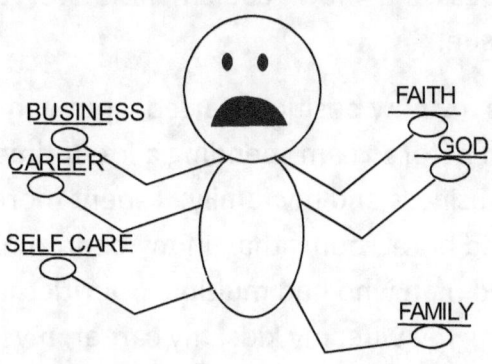

I have mentioned before that June 1st, 2018, was a big day for me. I signed a five-year lease that will soon become my flagship family entertainment center location. I also signed a sales contract to purchase an existing company from an owner that would have been my only competition in the area. If that wasn't busy enough, that same day, I was promoted to a new position at the company I worked for (I called it my 9 to 5 job). Before my promotion at my job, I had a good mix of work-life balance. I had enough time to run my business and have a full-time job. Around the same time I was forming my LLC, I was asked if I wanted to take a higher position in the 9 to 5 job. I knew that more responsibility meant a lot more hours. I also knew that this was a job that required significant travel. This was not the position I needed while trying to start my company. So, I said no to the promotion. Nah, just kidding. Do you honestly think that I would say that? I just took another drink of my awesomeness and knew I could handle everything without issue.

As soon as my new position started, I put in more hours than before. I am spending a lot of time away from my business and my family. I spent more time in airports and hotel rooms than in my bedroom. I was a 38-year-old man who had multiple priorities in life. I was juggling my wife, my kids, my career, my purchased business, and the tasks needed to launch in my new location. It didn't take more than a couple of weeks into June when things became overwhelming. I didn't mention anything, though. I didn't want to show any signs of losing control. I just kept on going.

I made it through the summer and was ready to launch my soon-to-be flagship location. I had hit all the tollgates I needed to make the building ready. I had spent 40 to 50 hours per week inside this building or at my purchased location, ensuring everything was running correctly. This is on top of the 50 to 60 hours per week I was putting in at my career and trying to carve out some time for family. That carving out time for the family quickly disintegrated into no time for family, friends, or God. Honestly, I did not put too much emphasis on not having space for family, friends, or faith. I just figured this was a temporary sacrifice, and I'll be able to catch up when I am rich and financially free.

By the end of summer, my company became the most important thing in my life. I started to see all the areas I have been juggling shrink. This was not a good thing. I began to regress in my career. My management always highly regarded me, but I started to miss on deliverables, and they have seen a significant reduction in effort in my career. In November 2018, after several coaching sessions with my boss, I was delivered a final "Come to Jesus" moment. My boss had told me that if she did not see a noticeable improvement in my work, she would be forced to let me go. While I was still confident that my company would be a huge success and that I would not need another career for much longer, I also knew that I still needed to be employed at that time. So, I started to shift focus away from my company and into my career.

I figured I already launched the business, and it was running fine. I would leave it to my employees to run, and they would follow directions as if I were there. They would care about my company as much as I would, right? Wrong! As soon as I took my eyes off the business, I noticed increased employee hours, office supplies, and snack bar expenses. I also saw an increase in customer complaints. No employee will care about your business as much as you do. Knowing that I couldn't take my foot off the gas in my career, I still had to do something to get my business back on track. So, I just decided to work harder and longer. I never took time off. I was either running an organization for my career or running my own business. This quickly made me realize that I did not own a company. I owned another job. That's right, I went into debt to own a job paying me nothing. I knew this wasn't how everything was supposed to go, but I was still sure that if I worked hard enough, I could push through this. There is free time on the other side of success.

Even though I didn't put much emphasis on spending time with family, it still was a space that I knew I was neglecting. In my mind, neglecting meant failing, and failing was something that I didn't do. So again, I tried to do it all. Run my company, have time with my family, have a career, and still have time to revel in my success. What ended up happening was years of poorly managed business financials, a termination from my job, and numerous missed sports games with the kids and dates with my wife. I tried balancing everything, but I couldn't hold on to anything.

It is possible to have a career and run a business. It would be best if you were clear on your priorities before you start that journey. My priorities were Business, Career, Family, Friends, and God. At the beginning of this book, I said everything here is strictly opinion and that what didn't work for me may work for you, but I lied. Because if you have priorities that match or come close to matching mine. You will ultimately fail. God should be the priority in your life. If He directs your life to His will, everything else will fall into place. Make time for your Faith and your Family. If your career and business aspirations would cause you to limit either of those, you may want to seek a new path.

DON'T LOSE SIGHT OF WHAT'S IMPORTANT IN YOUR LIFE

Failure #5: Not Understanding Building and Operating Costs:

BUILDING AND OPERATIONAL EXPENSES

I was very confident when creating my building and operating cost forecasts in my business plan. I knew what my rent would be. I understood the taxes were relatively high, but I only had to pay them out two times a year, so there was no need to budget monthly. I figured I would need around $2,000 monthly for electricity and heat and probably $50 to $100 monthly for water and sewer. The other operating costs would only be tablecloths and party supplies. I remember thinking that this should be easy. The problem was that I was making these building costs up. When I said "I figured," it meant I just guessed.

In reality, the building cost me more upfront and long-term costs. The day I signed the lease, I was told to bring a check with me for $24,000. I was not expecting this at all. I asked why, and they required this as a security deposit at the beginning of all leases. I also noticed that it was warm inside the building. When I started looking at the HVAC units, it didn't seem like many were working. Part of this lease agreement was that I would be 100% responsible for building repairs or upkeep. You would have thought a person as "skilled and clever" as I was would have had the building inspected before jumping into this lease, but you were wrong. Since I was now responsible for all repairs, I had our rooftop HVAC units serviced and repaired. The total bill for this was $10,000. So now I am $34,000 more into this building than I first planned. On top of that, it never occurred to me that my rent would be due on the 1st of each month after the lease was signed. I thought I wouldn't start paying rent until we opened and had revenue to cover it. Nope, that is not the case. I had to pay out $8,000 in rent for July, August, and September. That was an additional $24,000 in rent before any revenue was produced. By September 1st, I had spent $64,000 in unplanned building costs. Since this was not a budgeted expense, I had to use money from the start-up funds.

I was extremely mad at all these unplanned expenses that "happened" to me. I mean, it wasn't because of my poor planning or anything. It was just fate or bad luck. It was over now. The bills had been paid, and I could open my business and start making money. The new location opened on September 8th, 2018, and immediately started making money. The problem was that my operational expenses were rising faster than my revenue. I severely underestimated my monthly utility expenses. To make things worse, there were expenses that I needed to have that I never budgeted for. Expenses like the Internet, Phone, Point of Sale Fees, Credit Card Fees, and TV were missed from my original forecast. While I did plan for insurance, I only planned for liability. I didn't realize that as a leaseholder, I needed to provide building and property insurance, too.

Monthly Building and Operating Expenses

Expense	Planned Cost	Actual Cost
Monthly Rent	$ 8,000.00	$ 8,000.00
Water & Sewer	$ 50.00	$ 650.00
Electricty	$ 2,000.00	$ 4,500.00
Building Maintenance	$ 500.00	$ 800.00
Point of Sale Monthly Fees	Not Budgeted	$250.00
Credit Card Monthly Fees	Not Budgeted	$300.00
Insurances	$ 1,000.00	$ 1,800.00
Internet & Phone	Not Budgeted	$ 200.00
Office Expenses	$ 800.00	$ 1,000.00
Operating Supplies	$ 1,000.00	$ 1,200.00
Total Building & Operating Expenses	$ 13,350.00	$18,700.00

That $2,000 monthly electricity bill that I planned for was less than half of the actual costs most months. The HVAC units I spent $8,000 to repair are over 30 years old and use more energy than a rocket ship heading to the moon. I thought I was over budgeting for building maintenance. I thought that would be a few bucks here and there for paint or a vacuum cleaner. But we live in Pennsylvania. What happens in Pennsylvania from May through September? It is hot, and the grass grows. What happens in Pennsylvania from October through April? It is cold and snowy. I never thought I would need someone to plow and salt my parking lots in winter and mow and maintain our lawn in the summertime. Well, I should have because it is EXPENSIVE! I spent at least $ 3,000 yearly on snow removal and lawn care.

I spent over $5,000 more monthly on building and operational expenses than originally planned. That's over $60,000 more per year! This underestimation in planning would have never been noticed if my revenue numbers had come out as planned. Still, as you saw in a previous chapter, those planned revenue numbers were nothing more than a pipe dream.

This section is full of regrets. I should have asked more questions. I should have asked the building owner for copies of their utility bills over the prior twelve months. I should have paid for a building inspector to come in and expect the property before signing the lease. I should have negotiated a "construction" period in the lease where I would have the first three months of the lease rent-free and negotiated a smaller security deposit. My biggest regret was that I shouldn't have relied on my understanding and ego. I should have contacted people who have done this before to recognize better what expenses I may have missed in my original plan.

KNOW YOUR BUILDING AND OPERATING EXPENSES INTIMATELY!

Failure #6: Not Understanding Building Codes and Zoning Laws:

August 14th, 2018, is a day that will forever be burnt into my brain. My new location was wrapping up its final pieces of construction. We had our birthday party rooms built, our entryway walls installed, and our carpet was about to be laid. Everything was going great, and we were heading toward our September 1st launch! I was in Tampa, Florida, working at my 9-to-5 job when I received a phone call. It was the city's codes and zoning officer. Before this phone call, I never knew there was such a person. I know now that there is because he was on the other end of the line, and he was not happy. He told me that I was in violation of city ordinates and that I needed to cease construction immediately. I asked him why, and he told me that I never applied to change the building to the proper zone; I never applied for any permit or submitted drawings for the building to be reviewed and approved.

I still had no clue what he was talking about, but I did have drawings I created on my computer to show how the layout of the building would go. I sent that to him and was shot down right away. He needed official drawings signed by a licensed architect. What? Why wasn't my drawings good enough? They were perfect to scale and had much detail. Still, he made this a requirement, so as soon as I flew home on August 16th, I met an architect at the building and walked him through all he needed to be able to put the drawing together. While my architect completed my building plans, I applied for my zoning change and building permits.

When the code officer reviewed the official drawings, he put a maximum occupancy level of 1,300 people! Because our business needed to be zoned as an Assembly, a 1,300 max occupancy level meant I would need the correct number of bathrooms, parking spaces, drinking fountains, and service sinks, as seen below:

Facilities Required for Code Approval at 1,300 Max Occ

Item	Building Has	Code Requirement
Toilet Male	3	5
Toilet Female	3	10
Lavatories	2	7
Drinking Fountain	2	3
Service Sinks	1	3
Parking Spaces	95	325

There was no way I could pull this one off financially. To build that many extra toilets and fountains would cost over $100,000. Even if I was to complete that, the property only had 95 parking spaces. I couldn't have 230 additional parking spaces magically appear.

I know this book is meant to talk about everything I did wrong, but this next part highlights something I did right. I was furious when I heard about all of the coding requirements that needed to be done to open up. How is this possible? I knew that a business like mine would never have more than 150 people in it at one time. I wanted to rip the code officer a new one over the phone. I was just about to lay into him, but then I realized this was my fault. I never looked into this stuff before, and this poor guy is just trying to do his job. I was sure that 95% of his time is spent getting yelled at by people who think the laws around coding don't apply to them. It had to be a very thankless job. Instead of losing my cool, I told him I was sorry for not thinking about this. I understood he was doing his job and thanked him for getting back to me quickly. I always believed there was a solution to every problem, so I explained my situation and asked if he would work with me to find a solution. Once he realized he would not get berated with insults, he loosened up, and we started to talk more about my business. He told me he labeled my entire floor plan as a waiting area because he didn't understand what would happen there and that waiting areas hold a higher people per square foot ratio than most other work areas. I could take what I learned and go back to my architect to redo the drawings to include all the areas that would be used. For example, the architect labeled and calculated the square footage of the party rooms, parents' lounge, office space, and storage areas on the drawing. We resubmitted the plan to the codes officer at the end of August. He knew I had a planned start date of September 1st and tried to put a rush on the review, but he could not have them approved in time. With the new revisions to the layout, we got the maximum occupancy down to 385 people. This moved the required facilities for the building down to what was currently there, and we got the proper permits signed and approved for our Zoning and Construction plans on September 5th and had our official launch on September 8th.

I had advertised the entire month leading up to our launch that we would be open for business on September 1st. I sat down there on the 1st, greeting people and children as they walked into our doors, only to disappoint them and tell them we could not open that day. Two hundred ninety-five children came through those doors on the 1st and another 150 on the 2nd, only to be turned away. Not being able to open that weekend cost us over $5,000 in revenue. When you add this to the $7,500 architect bill from doing all of the last-minute and multiple revisions, my "Opening Weekend" cost me over $12,000. While this sucked big time, it could have been a lot worse if I didn't choose to be polite and respectful to the code officer. So take that as a side note. Never disrespect someone who can keep your building shut down!

This never would have been the case had I done more research to understand the building requirements for an operation like mine. I was so focused on picking out the right color of the carpet and creating our logo that I missed the entire code step. Again, I was lucky because if I hadn't found a solution for the code issue, I would be stuck in a five-year lease that was personally guaranteed with my home.

DO NOT SIGN A LEASE OR START CONSTRUCTION WITHOUT UNDERSTANDING YOUR BUSINESS' CODE AND ZONING REQUIREMENTS!

Failure #7: Overspending on Non-Essentials:

Even though launching my business ended up in a complete disaster that left me broke and possibly homeless, I must admit that setting up our new location was the most fun time I had in this process. In my head, I was already seeing my brand as a nationally recognized brand. Because I wanted my brand and logo to be recognizable, I wanted to ensure it was everywhere.

Most of my business was indoor inflatable bounce houses and obstacle courses. I had it in my plan to purchase at least 10 of these to start my business off. I initially set aside $60,000 for new inflatable equipment in the start-up budget. The problem I faced was that I didn't have enough left in my start-up funds to cover $60,000 in equipment. When it came time to place the orders for my new bounce houses, I was pleasantly pleased to see that the inflatable cost was not as high as I expected. I could have purchased the ten inflatables for a little over $40,000. To get that price, I would need to take the inflatables in their normal, generic mode. Traditionally, they use red, yellow, and blue colors with no specific logos. I didn't want to be generic. I wanted my business to be known throughout the land! Generic bounce houses do not show the level of success and professionalism that I (more like my ego) wanted to convey. So I asked for a quote to get them all colored with my company's colors and branded with my company's logo everywhere. They gave me a comparison quote so I could see what the cost would be "As Is," meaning using the generic print, and what the cost would be if I had them custom-made:

Costs of Custom Made Bounce Houses

Item	Cost "As IS"	Custom Cost
Tiger Bounce	$ 3,700.00	$ 4,900.00
50' Obstacle Course	$ 6,700.00	$ 9,500.00
Combo Bounce	$ 3,500.00	$ 4,700.00
Large Obstacle Course	$ 5,500.00	$ 8,300.00
Corner Bounce	$ 5,500.00	$ 8,300.00
Palm Tree Bounce	$ 2,500.00	$ 4,100.00
Zoo Themed Bounce	$ 2,700.00	$ 4,300.00
Double Slide Combo	$ 5,500.00	$ 8,300.00
20' Obstacle Course	$ 5,200.00	$ 7,900.00
Castle Bounce	$ 2,500.00	$ 4,100.00
Total Spend	$ 43,300.00	$ 64,400.00

The cost to customize my equipment was $21,100 more than if I wanted to accept them with the generic colors.

I did not have $64,400 on equipment, but I wanted them to show my logo. I wanted them to be my colors. After all, the kids would prefer to jump on customized, branded inflatables instead of the normal red, yellow, and blue ones. Right? I talked myself into it, and these ten inflatables were being produced precisely how I wanted them to be! The salesperson selling me all this customized equipment could sense the opportunity for easy sales because she jumped into advertising. How are people going to know where my business is? I needed something that would stand out and be seen from the highway. So, for only $4,000, I had that manufacturing company give me a 10-foot and 20-foot inflatable version of my mascot. Notice how I said, "Only $4,000". That is because they said the regular price was $6,000. Now, I could pat myself on the back for saving $2,000! I still didn't have enough money in my start-up budget to purchase this custom-made equipment, though. I reminded myself of the old saying, "You gotta spend money to make money." While I know this is not a true statement now, I lived by it back then. I returned to my savings and pulled another $50,000 for the custom equipment. Man, I was really dumb!

I didn't stop at my inflatable equipment. Over the summer, I was branding everything with my logo. Pens, Notebooks, Boom-a-range, Water Bottles, and T-shirts were all ordered with my branded logo. The lowest point was spending $13 per unit on coffee cups with my logo. You couldn't sell them for $6, but here I am, spending $13 to have them made. I was out of control.

I will be honest: when I turned on those inflatables, which showed our bright colors and logo, it looked cool. My 20-foot inflatable mascot on the building's roof towered over the area. Everyone knew where my business was. It looked sharp and professional. It gave the impression that we were not just a small business. We were a household brand, like Nike or Coca-Cola. I watched as children went in and out of them, bouncing until they could not bounce anymore. Knowing I made the right call to spend that extra money branding my equipment was an incredible feeling. But did I really make the right call?

In 2020, I purchased four used bounce houses from a competitor. These bounce houses were the standard red, yellow, and blue colors and had no specific branding. They didn't look as sharp or professional as mine did. They looked dull and ugly. I put them up inside of my building, and guess what happened? The same children I saw going in and out of my beautiful custom bounce houses were going in and out of these generic ones. It turns out that the kids don't give a hoot about the color or the inflatables. They didn't care if it had a fancy logo printed on it. All they cared about was if it was full of air so they could jump and slide. About two weeks after we launched, I stopped turning on that expensive 20-foot inflatable mascot. Do you think people stopped coming in? Nope. People were still able to find us and still kept coming in daily.

I spent money I didn't have on stuff I didn't need. That money could have been used to help us through our upcoming slow season. It could have been used to pay down debt. For all I knew, it could have been used to take my family on a vacation. Those options would have provided more return value than spending on unneeded branding.

It is a good thing to get your brand out there. Just make sure you are not just dumping money into something that will deliver you no return. I should have been spending my money more wisely, focused on putting my money into parts of the business that would give me a payback.

DON'T SPEND A LOT OF MONEY ON THINGS THAT WILL DELIVER YOU NO RETURN!

Failure #8: Not Managing Employee Costs:

As a parent, I knew that the safety and cleanliness of my new building would be two of the most significant factors to impact my business. To ensure the parents knew that I was equally concerned about their children's safety and the equipment's cleanliness, I planned to fill my building with as many staff members as possible. I had 25 staff members hired for the day one launch.

From operating my existing location through the summer, I started to understand what days of the week had the highest percentage of customers. This family entertainment center brought in nearly 70% of its revenue across Friday, Saturday, and Sunday. I used this to staff my new building. Mondays through Thursdays, I would have two staff members on-site during our hours of operation (10 a.m. to 7 p.m.). On Fridays, I would still have two staff members there from 10 a.m. to 3 p.m., but I would increase my staff numbers to 5 from 3 p.m. to when we closed at 9 p.m. to account for families coming to play after school. On Saturdays and Sundays, I would schedule nearly everyone on the roster to work at least 4 hours daily. This would give me the most amount of employee presence when we needed it the most. There were times on a Saturday when I had as many as 14 staff members working at one time.

I kept this system going through April 2019, when my first "busy season" ended. Honestly, I never paid that much attention to what I was paying out to my employees during this time because I was too focused on how much revenue was coming in! It wasn't until the revenue was cut in half in April and my business account didn't have much money in it that I looked into the impact the employee costs had on my bottom line. I started pulling quarterly snapshots of revenue versus employee costs. What I found left me sick to my stomach:

Company Expenses

	Q4 2018	Q1 2019	Total
Total Revenue	$ 83,700.56	$ 94,568.77	$ 178,269.33
Total Employee Hours	3,441.73	3,785.50	$ 7,227.23
Total Employee Wage	$ 28,084.52	$ 30,889.68	$ 58,974.20
Total Employer Tax	$ 3,426.31	$ 3,768.54	$ 7,194.85
Total Employee Cost	$ 31,510.83	$ 34,658.22	$ 66,169.05
% Employee Cost to Rev	38%	37%	37%

This whole time, I was patting myself on the back because of that fat revenue. I didn't even notice that almost 40% of everything I brought in was going back out to cover employee costs.

I remember thinking to myself, at least I put the customer first and ensured we had as many staff members on site as possible to help keep their children safe. It may cost more, but surely, more must be better. Correct? Like so many other times in this journey, I was wrong. Just having more people does not make the business better. Economist Jacques Turgot is credited for articulating the Law of Diminishing Returns. This economic principle states that as an investment increases, the rate of return on that investment, after a certain point, can't continue to increase.

In my situation, I was increasing my investment by increasing my floor staff and expecting continued increases in the cleanliness and safety of my operation. Thus increasing my customer's experience. While I received daily customer compliments on how safe and clean our facility was, I also noticed our employees while they worked. Some were out on the floor, cleaning, playing with kids, and interacting with parents. Then there were also several just standing around like they didn't have much to do. These staff members who were not doing anything were also catching the parents' attention. I started getting complaints and poor reviews because they thought my staff was not engaging enough. This was the total opposite result that I had expected. Now, I know that these staff members who were accused of not being engaged could have taken some initiative and found something productive to do, but their lack of work was created by having too many people working at one time. There was not enough work to do for the staff I had on schedule. Those extra people provided little to no value to the operation then. Because I received complaints due to the perception of "lazy" workers, those additional people provided a negative value to my business.

I started correcting this mistake right away. I didn't want to slash staffing immediately without knowing what I was looking for. Instead, I gradually pulled back on scheduled staff each month to see where my optimal staffing plan should be. Eventually, I was able to find my optimal staffing levels, and as you can see in the table below, I was able to reduce our employee cost to revenue percentage from 37% down to 23%

Company Expenses

	Q4 2022	Q1 2023	Total
Total Revenue	$ 64,160.61	$ 85,645.73	$ 149,806.34
Total Employee Hours	1,598.19	1,969.07	$ 3,567.26
Total Employee Wage	$ 13,665.03	$ 16,953.37	$ 30,618.40
Total Employer Tax	$ 1,431.95	$ 1,768.81	$ 3,200.76
Total Employee Cost	$ 15,096.98	$ 18,722.18	$ 33,819.16
% Employee Cost to Rev	24%	22%	23%

Despite the reduced staffing levels, I still received compliments about how clean and safe my facility was. I'm not saying that you must always run a skeleton crew. Do not sacrifice your company's reputation to save a few hundred bucks in pay, but you need to know your tipping point between being understaffed, right-staffed, or overstaffed.

I know that learning this is all part of what a business owner goes through, but my lack of attention in this matter cost me over $100,000 in unneeded employee costs until I could find the right mix.

DO NOT OVERSTUFF YOUR OPERATION

Failure #9: Not Planning for the Slow Season:

From the very start, my research told me that my business would have a busy and slower season. Since we were an indoor facility in the northeastern part of the country, my busy season was when it started to get cold out. This "busy" season usually started in middle to late October and ran to early April. From May through September, I was at the mercy of the weather gods. If it were nice out, I would be slow. If it were rainy, I would be packed. I never really understood how much of a drop off in revenue the slow season could bring, though.

My first experience with the "slow" time happened when I purchased the existing business on June 1st, 2018. That summer turned out to be one of the wettest summers on record. It rained almost every other day for three months. Because of this rain, people kept coming in to play. I remember seeing my July revenue numbers; they looked like numbers I would expect to see in November. Man, I must be good at this business stuff. I wish I were joking, but I remember thinking that my superior business knowledge drew customers into my facility during what was supposed to be the slow season. It wasn't the daily monsoons coming through the area. Nope, it was all me.

We launched our new facility in September to be poised for the upcoming "busy" season. As I mentioned, we became an instant hit when we opened up—pulling in monthly revenues higher than anticipated. I had money left over at the end of each month. I thought most businesses struggle when they open, but here I am, having money left over at the end of the month! I am awesome at this!

I am so awesome at this that I knew our slow season would be minor. People would continue to come through my doors every day. I was honestly planning on having $30,000 or more in revenue every month of the year. Since I knew we would always have this money coming in, there was no need to worry about saving for slow time. I used the money to buy a new truck, take my family on trips, and purchase stuff for my home. I even wanted to prove how awesome of an owner I was and paid for a Christmas Party that was professionally catered. Yep, I was showing all the outward signs of success. The busy season continued its progression until March 2019, when we hit our highest revenue month. It was so high that I planned to retire by the end of 2019 and be a full-time business owner.

It was April 2019, and I was excited to see how much we would make this month. There wasn't much money in my business account because of mismanaging employee costs and building expenses. Plus, if there was anything else left, I just spent it as if it was petty cash. I knew I had a $14,000 property tax bill due that month, but I was not worried. My business would generate that in a week, and I would be ready.

As it turned out, April provided uncharacteristically rain-free days. No rain at all. Just beautiful warm and sunny weather. It was a much-welcomed site for us northerners cramped inside during the winter. It was as if someone flipped off a light switch; my business went from boom to bust overnight. I went from having a surplus of cash at the end of each month to being unable to pay all my bills with the money we brought in. So, again, I had to go back to my savings or what was left to cover the losses.

That entire summer was simply perfect weather. Beautiful sunny weather all day long and a small shower overnight. It was a farmer's dream, but it was my nightmare. I struggled that entire summer. Several times, I returned to my savings to help pay the bills. When my savings ran out, I got another loan from my bank. I had to get another loan when my

$18,000 school tax bill came due in August. Only this one wasn't from a bank. It was from one of those "same-day deposit" loan companies. The ones that charge huge fees. They are the modern-day loan sharks. I received $18,000 from them in August and paid them back at $6,000 monthly for the next four months. So that $18,000 tax bill ended up costing me $24,000.

Finally! Its October! It's time for our busy season to start! I saw a quick uptick in customer traffic, which drove our revenue back up to more comfortable levels. I had learned my lesson and was ready to save for the slow season this time. I am sure I will get back on track and be that fantastic business owner I know I am. Not so fast. The additional loan I received from the bank and the short-term loan from the loan shark totaled an additional $7,500 in monthly bills. With these additional bills included, I was left with no money at the end of each month. The final installment was paid to the loan shark in January 2020. Just in time to hear about a new virus causing a lot of trouble worldwide. Yep, that next month, COVID hit the United States, and my busy season was prematurely shut down, and I didn't have any more time to try and save up for the slow season.

While I did learn my lesson on saving for the slower seasons, I never recovered from the mistakes I made during my first six months in business at my flagship facility. The next few years were just a series of short-term loans and covering bills with my accounts. Those six months were the difference between having the cash to be totally out of debt now and being stuck under a mountain of debt that will take decades to pay off.

If I could reset the clock and go back, I would have treated any money produced by the business as money I could not touch. I would have put it into a figurative vault and thrown away the key. I had no right to touch any of that money. I should've created a separate account and moved any monthly surplus into it. This would keep the business afloat during the slow months. Instead, I treated my business like it was my ATM. Your business might not have a slow season. That is great, but I would still plan for one. A slow season might not be a few months. It might be some unexpected construction in front of your building that is keeping customers away. It might be a shortage of raw materials used in your product that halts production.   It really could be anything that would keep you from selling your product. Please don't get caught like I did.

DO NOT TOUCH THAT MONEY! PLAN FOR THE SLOW SEASON!

Failure #10: Giving Too Much Away:

The customer is always right! No "Ifs", "Ands", or "Buts"! This was my mantra when I launched my company. My vision was to have a company that is so customer-centric that parents would want to come in as bad as their children. I wanted everyone who came through my doors to leave happy and satisfied with their experience. If, for some weird reason, someone was unhappy with their experience, I would do anything it took to make it right. This chapter was challenging for me to write because I believe that for a business to survive, you need to be customer-focused, and a business owner needs to be in tune with how the customers feel about your business. However, I believe I took these principles to an extreme in my business.

I saw hundreds of children coming in as paid admissions and another couple hundred children as part of weekly birthday parties. Because I always required at least one parent or guardian to accompany a child in my facility, and when you include parents, it was not a stretch for my locations to have thousands of customers each week. When you have that many people coming in every week, ensuring everyone has the best possible experience is nearly impossible. Well, it's almost impossible for any other business owner than me. I knew that I could always keep my company at the highest reputation, and I would do anything to make any issues right.

I ensured that my business cards were placed on the reception desk at my locations. These cards included my cell phone number. I did this so my customers could get a hold of me anytime. It didn't take long before I started to receive phone calls from customers. I always listened to each person's issues and responded apologetically, even when things were beyond my control or downright silly. I had no idea how petty and demanding some of my customers were. Some of the "issues" people had were:

"There were too many people in the building."

"The Philadelphia Eagles were on the TV instead of the Pittsburgh Steelers."

"My party started at 2:00 PM, but when I arrived at 1:15 PM, I couldn't get into the party room."

"One of your staff members looked at me funny."

"My child cried when we were getting ready to leave because he didn't want to go. You should have some stickers or candy available to bribe kids to leave. This is unacceptable."

"Another child said something mean to my child."

"I only stayed for about an hour. Why should I have paid full price?"

"I wanted to have a party without using your rooms, but your manager told me I couldn't. I know your rules show that you can only have parties in the reserved party rooms, but my kid should be different."

These examples were just a fraction of the calls I received weekly. While there were some legitimate opportunities I could take action on with my staff and processes, most were complaints from people looking to get their money back. They all threatened me with a one-star review on my social media sites. To me, a one-star review would be the same as someone taking a match to my building. I couldn't have that at all.

So, I caved. I started apologizing to everyone who called to make a complaint. I told them that my goal was always to ensure everyone's satisfaction and that I would make it right. Without investigating the validity of their grumbles, I began issuing partial or full refunds to my customers. I thought I was doing right by my customers, but as it turned out, I was being taken advantage of. After about four or five months in business, I discovered that I had gained a reputation as a business that would refund your purchases. All you had to do was call. It wasn't uncommon for one of my locations to take in $4,000 on a Saturday but have $400 in refunded payments.

Always taking the customer's opinions as fact did not only negatively impact my financials. It also negatively impacted the morale of my staff. By mindlessly taking my customer's complaints as the actual account of what happened, I was discounting my staff's understanding of the incident. My staff did not feel supported by me, and I started to see attrition. I put a score on a social media page ahead of my team. I lost some good staff members in the first six months of operation because I was too focused on not receiving a one-star review. While customer service should have been a massive part of my priorities, I needed to realize that solutions to problems didn't always have to be by way of refunds. I created and posted procedures and processes for the customers to see when they entered the door. I needed to stick by these instead of making exceptions for those who felt the processes should not apply to them. I should have taken responsibility for the issues that were my fault and actionable, but not for people trying to nitpick to get something for free.

I started to correct this behavior in myself during the first quarter of 2019. I still listened to my customers but stood up for myself and my team when warranted. I stopped mindlessly giving out refunds for no reason. Obviously, some of the customers did not receive this well, and I got some one-star reviews. I was mortified seeing the one-star and the blurb explaining why my business was not worth going to anymore. I thought I was sunk. What I experienced next surprised me. I started seeing comments under these reviews from my other customers. They came to my defense! The customers were promoting my business, replying to the negative reviews. At that point, I realized the age-old saying, "You can't please everyone every time." I should have focused less of my time on the small percentage of people who were unhappy and poured more energy into the large number of people who loved my establishment.

Refunds were not the only way I failed because of giving too much away. I also gave money and gifts to charities and people who could not afford our services. This section may be confusing because I will contradict myself in my final chapter. I also want to make sure that I am very much in favor of giving your time and resources to charitable organizations and doing what you can to help your fellow man. As a business owner, you just need to decide your business. Is it a business, or is it a charity?

I made commitments that I would donate five percent of my profits each month to a local charity. I made this commitment publicly, and the charity I would be supporting that month was published right on the front page of my website. At the end of our first month, I reviewed my financials and noticed that I had lost several thousand dollars. This should have been acceptable, being a new business, but not to me. I didn't want people to think that I couldn't turn a profit in month one. So I pulled $1000 out of my personal savings and presented a check to a local Christian school so they could purchase new sports equipment. I wanted to ensure everyone knew how philanthropic I was, so I had the local newspaper there to take pictures. I used made-up profits to donate to charity to look like a generous, successful business person. This habit continued throughout the next five years. I had given away thousands of dollars to charities based on fake profits.

Now, giving to charities is not bad, but I did it for all the wrong reasons. I did it publicly, intending to create the perception of success. It was not just monthly donations. Anytime an organization would come to me about an event they were doing or a charity auction and ask for donations, I would always provide them with gift cards, admission passes, or free birthday parties as prize donations.

I also could not pull my personal feelings away when it came to families who could not afford much of our services. Several families reached out to book parties at my facility, but when they understood the price, they said they could not afford it. They told me how their child would be heartbroken now and if there was anything that I could do. I couldn't stand to see a child be turned away because of money, so that I would book a party room for them at a reduced or no cost.

Even after this post-mortem dives into my business, I would still do this for less fortunate children. This might make me a decent human being, but it makes me a terrible business owner. I wanted my business to be one of the most generous organizations in my area. Still, because I treated it more like a mission than a business, I could not have the financial capabilities to be around long enough for that to happen. I have heard people say business owners are all greedy and stingy with their money. I'm sure some are, but all business owners need to be frugal with their money so that they can be around to help people.

DON'T GIVE AWAY YOUR MONEY! DON'T TREAT YOUR BUSINESS LIKE A CHARITY

Conclusion:

This book was hard for me to write because it forced me to humble myself and see the damage my Ego had done to myself, my family, and the community. Because of my failures, 20 fantastic staff workers, many with families to support, no longer have a job. Because of my failures, my beautiful wife looks at me resentfully because I could not provide her with the secure and stable life she deserves. Because of my failures, my children will have to answer questions from their classmates about why they can't come and have fun in our facility anymore.

I know that this book might be received as an advertisement telling you not to start a business. This was not my intent. I love entrepreneurship! I loved owning a business that provided jobs to the community and a source of fun and exercise for the area's children. I just failed miserably in execution. I wanted to succeed so badly and worked tirelessly to make my success happen. The problem was that I let working hard seem more important than working smart.

Seriously, please don't read this and say business ownership isn't worth it. Being your own boss is one of the greatest feelings in the world and is definitely worth the risk and hard work it will take to get there.

Yes, it will take risks. Anything worth doing in life will have some level of risk, and while I did say that the end result of being your own boss is worth the risk, I urge you to understand those risks. Understand the impact those risks have on not just you but your family, friends, and other people you love. If you have a spouse or a partner, discuss these risks openly so there are no surprises. If either one of you feels that the risks that you would be taking far outweigh the rewards of success, please do not proceed. Work together and develop a new strategy involving less risk or greater reward. This may be as simple as aggressively saving for a year so you do not have to go into debt to start the business. Either way that you decide, you can proceed together and unified. Do not let your ego overtake your common sense. Do not force your business into existence. Deciding not to launch a business that you had been planning because the numbers didn't seem to line up or the market might not support the growth that you initially anticipated is not a sign of failure. It's a sign of intelligence and maturity.

Hard work alone will not make you a success. If it did, I would not be writing a book about being a failure. So take this book. Take this list of embarrassing failures I presented to you. Learn from my mistakes, make better decisions than I did, and launch your business the right way!

I will finish this book the way I started it. Hi, my name is J.D., and I am a failure. You, my friend, will be a success!

I would love to hear from you and your journey. Please reach out to me at CYEJDD@gmail.com. I will do whatever I can to help you build your business.